Easy Piano

HARRY STYLES
EASY PIANO COLLECTION

Photo by Handout/Helene Marie Pambrun via Getty Images

ISBN 978-1-70513-132-9

Visit Hal Leonard Online at
www.halleonard.com

Contact us:
Hal Leonard
7777 West Bluemound Road
Milwaukee, WI 53213
Email: info@halleonard.com

In Europe, contact:
Hal Leonard Europe Limited
42 Wigmore Street
Marylebone, London, W1U 2RN
Email: info@halleonardeurope.com

In Australia, contact:
Hal Leonard Australia Pty. Ltd.
4 Lentara Court
Cheltenham, Victoria, 3192 Australia
Email: info@halleonard.com.au

CONTENTS

ADORE YOU

Words and Music by HARRY STYLES,
THOMAS HULL, TYLER JOHNSON
and AMY ALLEN

Moderate Pop Rock

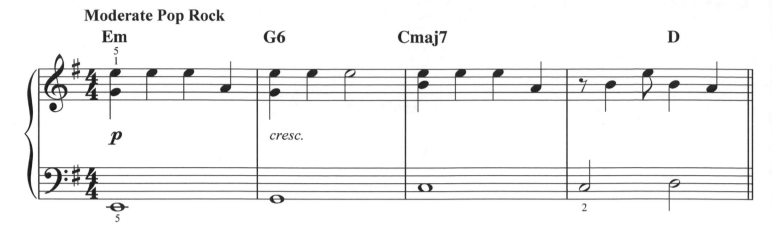

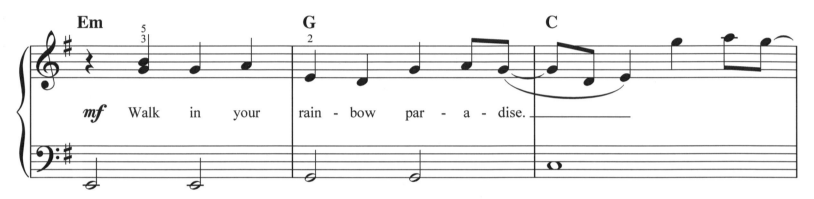

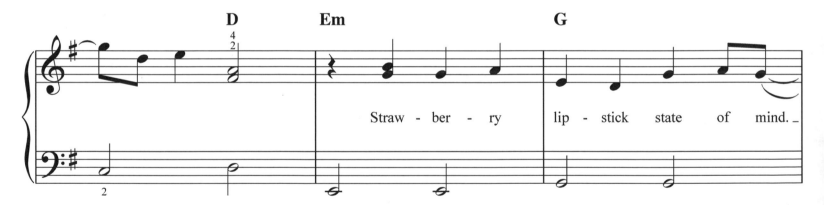

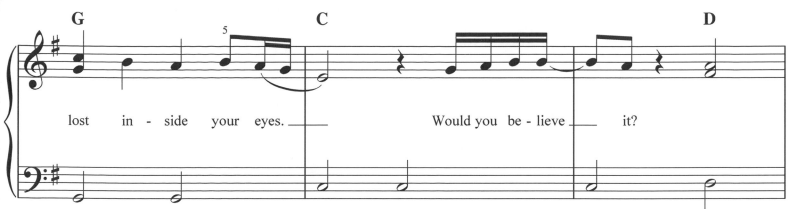

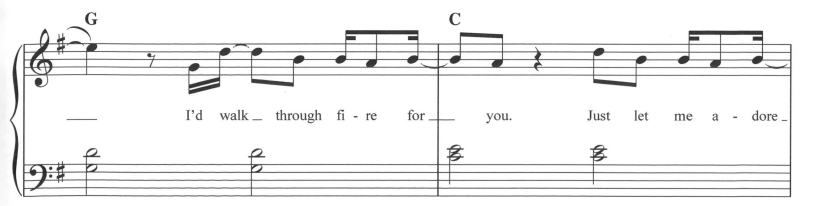

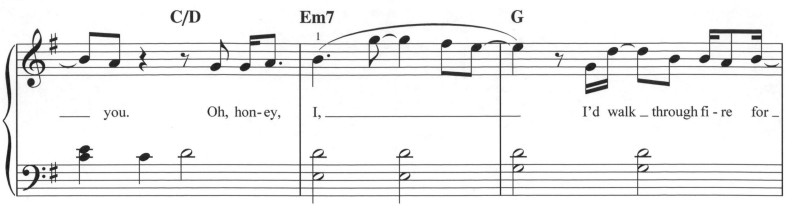

you.   Oh, hon-ey,   I, _____   I'd walk _ through fi - re   for _

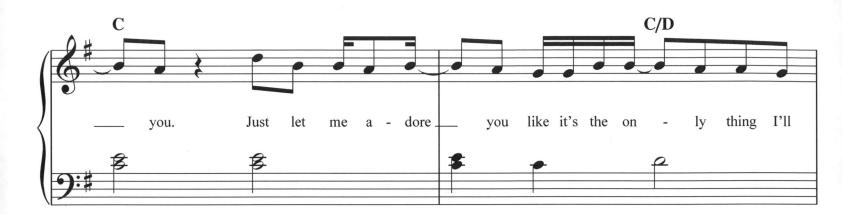

_____ you.   Just let me a-dore ___ you like it's the on - ly thing I'll

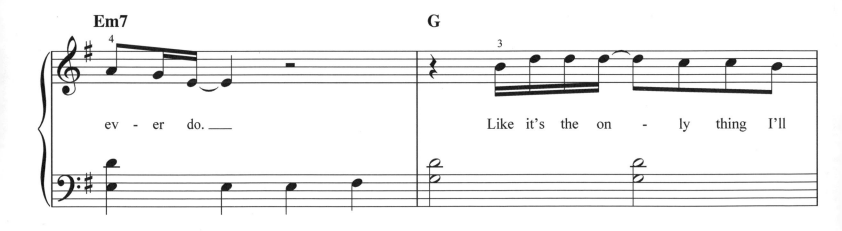

ev - er do. ___   Like it's the on - ly thing I'll

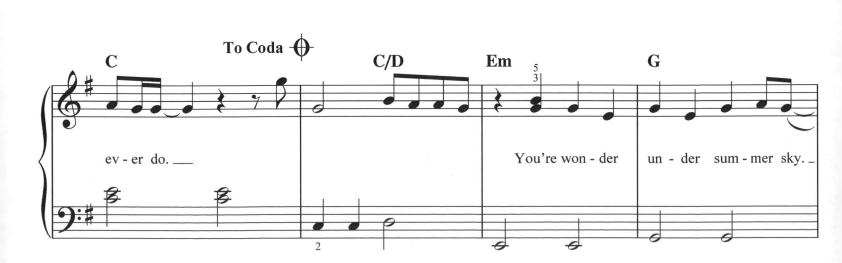

ev-er do. ___   You're won - der   un - der sum-mer sky. _

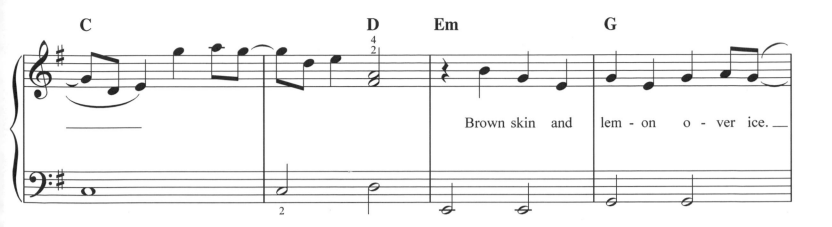

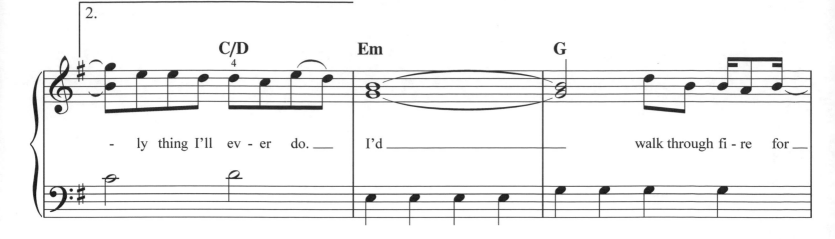

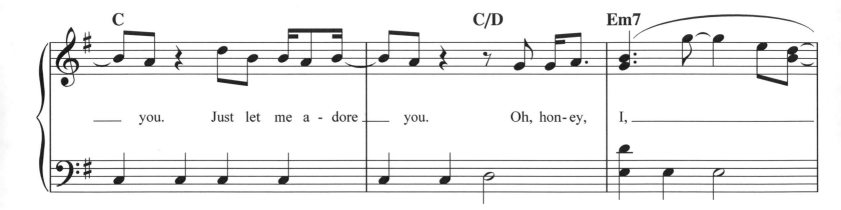

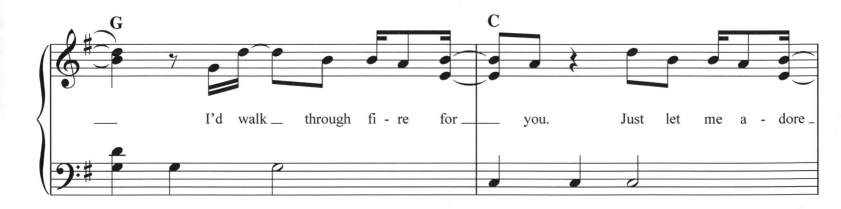

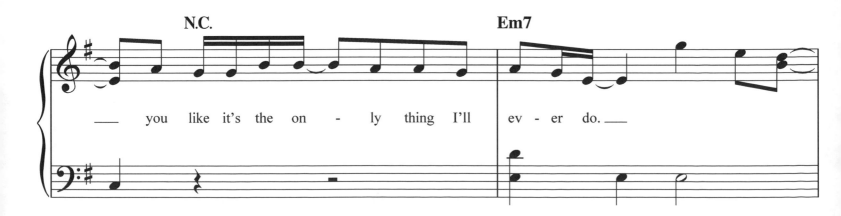

I'd walk _ through fi - re for ___ you. Just let me a - dore ___ you. Oh, hon - ey,

I, _____ I'd walk _ through fi - re for ___ you. Just let me a - dore _

___ you. Oh, hon - ey.

Just let me a - dore ___ you like it's the on - ly thing I'll ev - er do. _

CAROLINA

Words and Music by HARRY STYLES,
THOMAS HULL, JEFF BHASKER,
TYLER JOHNSON, ALEX SALIBIAN,
MITCH ROWLAND and RYAN NASCI

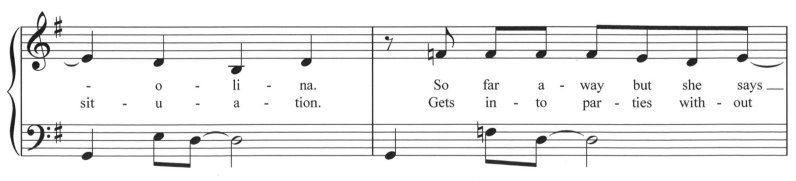

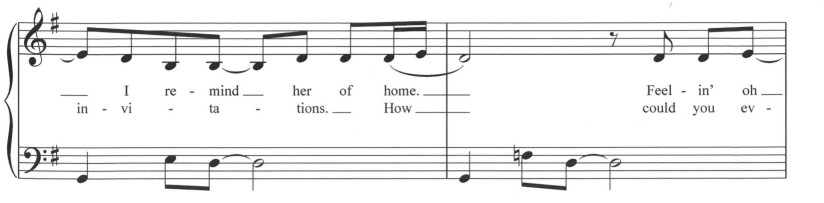

I re - mind her of home. Feel - in' oh
in - vi - ta - tions. How could you ev -

so far from home.
- er turn her down?

She nev - er saw her - self as a west coast - er.
There's not a drink that I think could sink her.

Moved all the way 'cause her grand - ma told her, "Townes,
How would I tell her that she's all I think a - bout?

bet - ter swim ___ be - fore you drown." ___
Well, I guess ___ she just found out. ___

A5　Bb5　C5　D5

She's a good girl. ___ She's such a

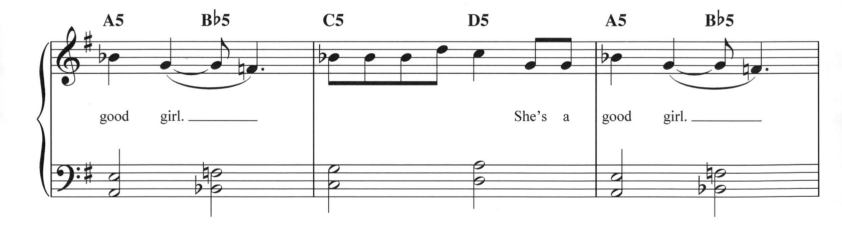

A5　Bb5　C5　D5　A5　Bb5

good girl. ___ She's a good girl. ___

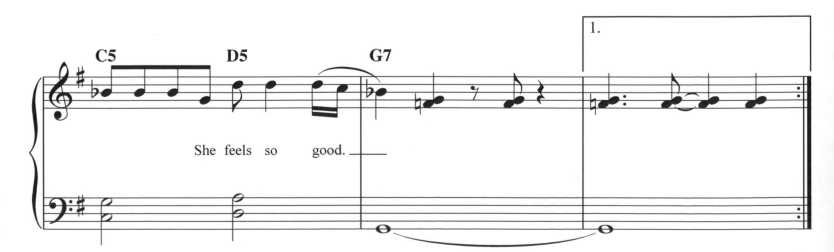

C5　D5　G7

1.

She feels so good. ___

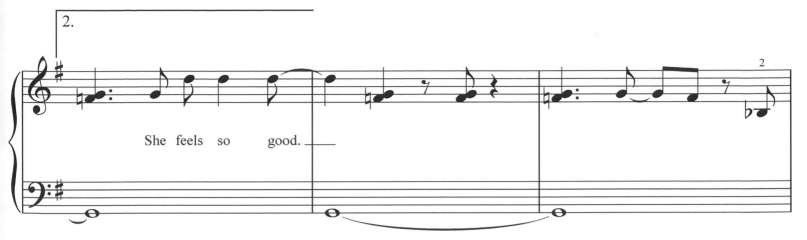

She feels so good.

I met her once and wrote a song a - bout her.

I wan-na scream. Yeah, I wan-na shout it out. And I hope

she hears me now.

Play 3 times

La la la la la la la _____ la la la.

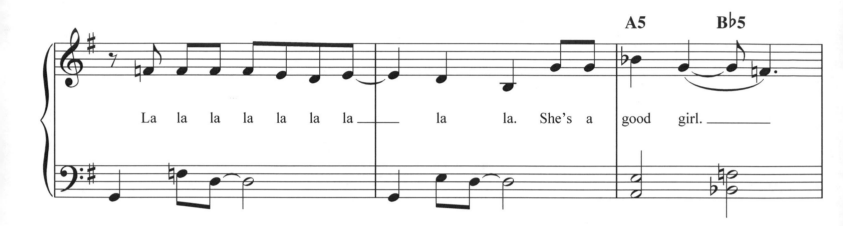

A5   B♭5

La la la la la la la _____ la la. She's a good girl. _____

C5   D5   A5   B♭5   C5   D5

She's such a good girl. _____ She's a

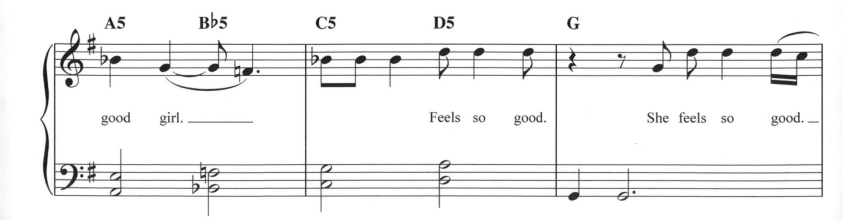

A5   B♭5   C5   D5   G

good girl. _____ Feels so good. She feels so good. _____

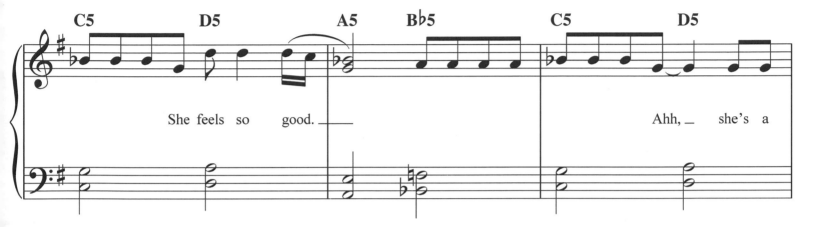

FALLING

Words and Music by HARRY STYLES
and THOMAS HULL

Lyrics:

I'm in my bed,

and you're not here.
you missed me, too.

And there's no
And I'm

G ... **Em7** ... **F**

one to blame ___ but the drink ___ and my wan - der - ing hands. ___
well a - ware ___ I write too ___ man - y songs ___ a - bout you. ___

C

For - get what I ___ said; ___ it's not what I ___ meant. ___
The cof - fee's ___ out ___ at Beach - wood Ca - fé. ___

Am7 ... **G**

And I can't ___ take it back, ___ I can't un -
And it kills ___ me, 'cause I ___ know we've run ___

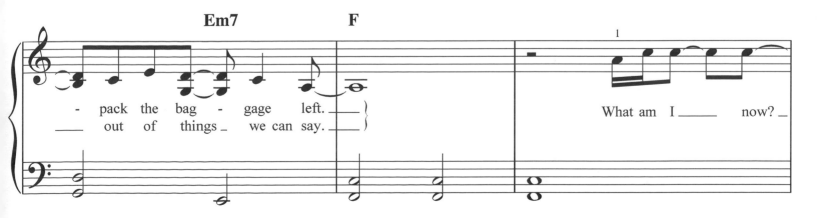

Em7 ... **F**

- pack the bag - gage left. ___
___ out of things ___ we can say. ___

What am I ___ now?

What am I ____ now? ____

{ 1., 2. What if I'm ____ some -
D.S. What if you're ____ some -

Am7

- one I don't ____ want a - round? ____
- one I just ____ want a - round? ____

I'm fall -

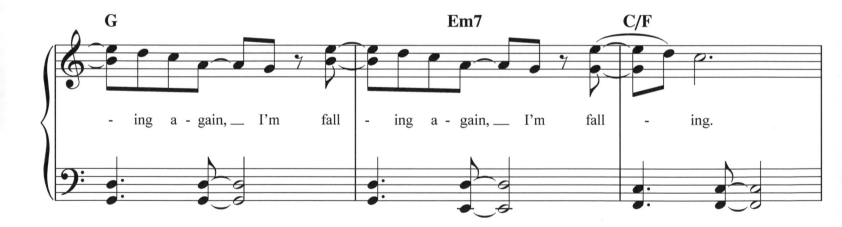

G   Em7   C/F

- ing a - gain, ____ I'm fall - ing a - gain, ____ I'm fall - ing.

C

What if I'm ____ down? ____   What if I'm ____ out? ____   What if I'm ____ some -

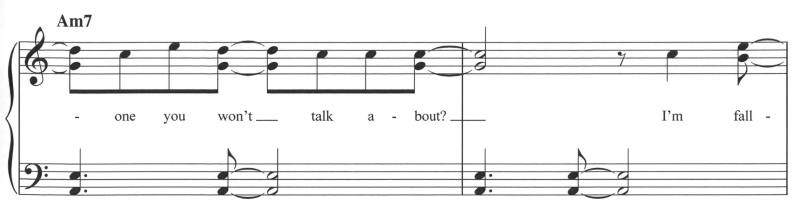

- one you won't ___ talk a - bout? ___ I'm fall -

- ing a - gain, ___ I'm fall - ing a - gain, ___ I'm fall - ing.

You said you cared, ___

I get ___ the feel - ing ___ that you'll nev - er need me ___ a -

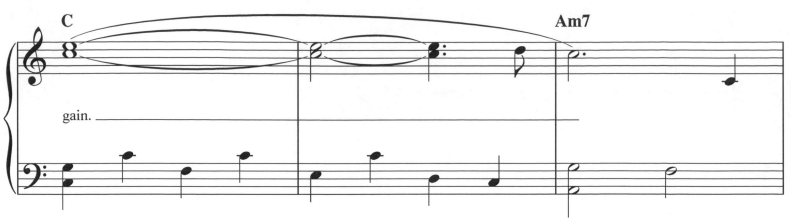

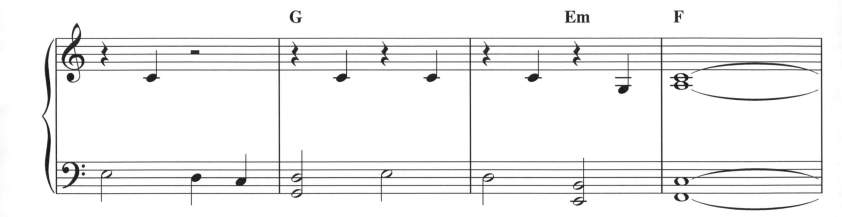

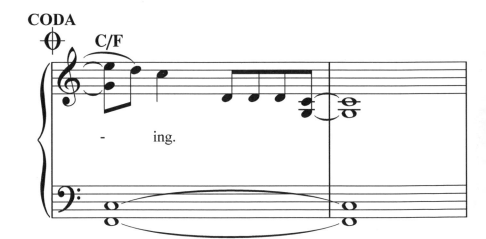

LIGHTS UP

Words and Music by HARRY STYLES,
THOMAS HULL and TYLER JOHNSON

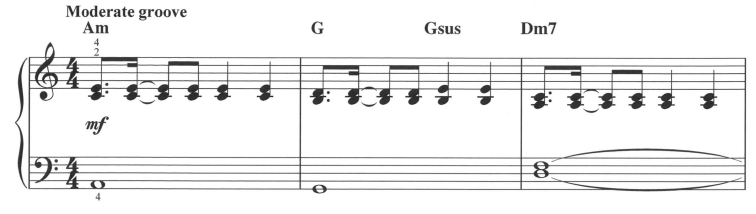

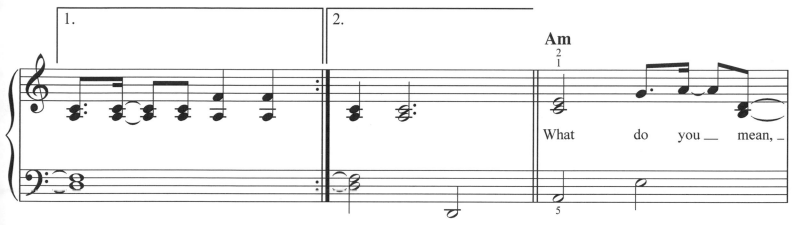

What do you __ mean, __

__ "I'm sor - ry, __ by __ the way." Nev - er com - ing back down. __

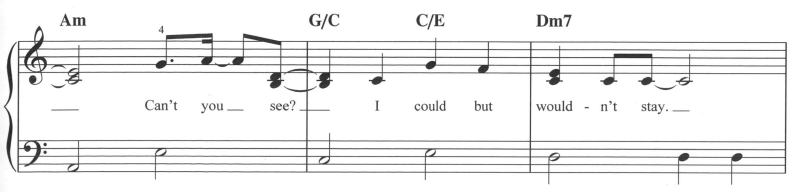

__ Can't you __ see? __ I could but would - n't stay. __

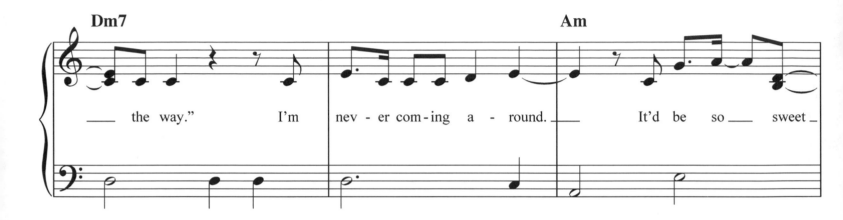

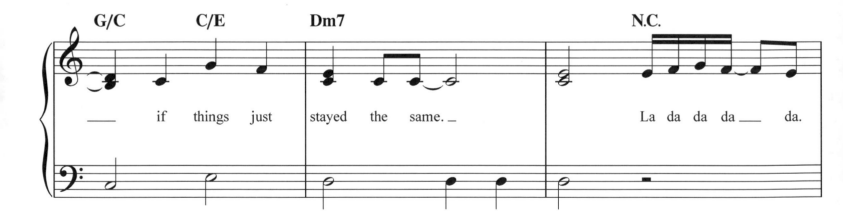

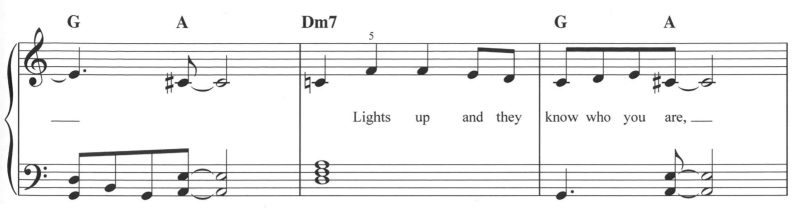

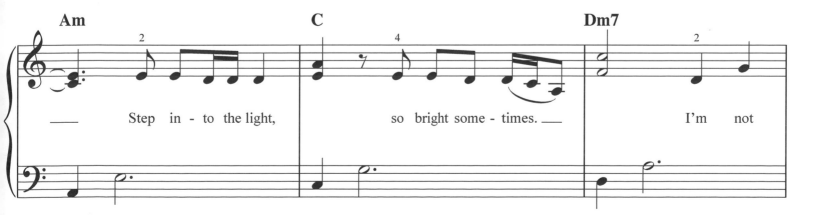

24

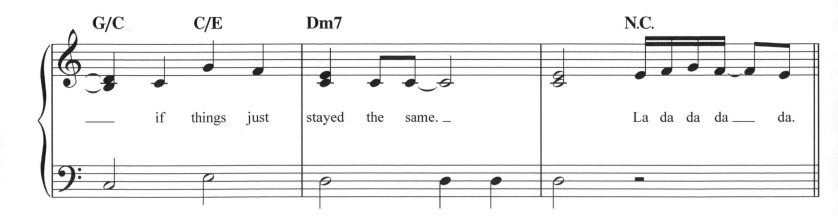

Play 3 times

La da da da ____ da. Oh. ____ La da da da ____ da.

Oh. ____ All the lights could-n't put out the dark ____

run-ning through my heart. ____ Lights up and they

know who you are, ____ know who you are. ____ Do you know who you are? ____

GOLDEN

Words and Music by HARRY STYLES,
THOMAS HULL, MITCHELL ROWLAND
and TYLER JOHNSON

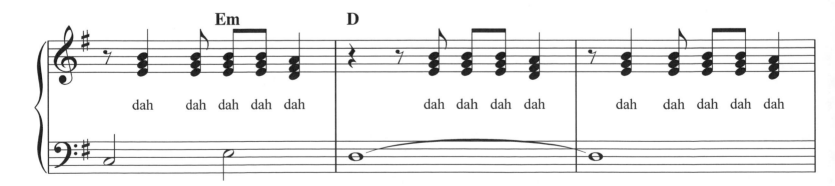

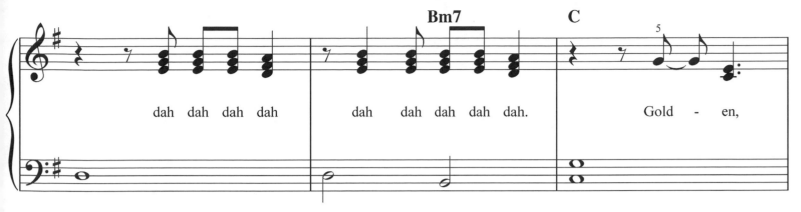

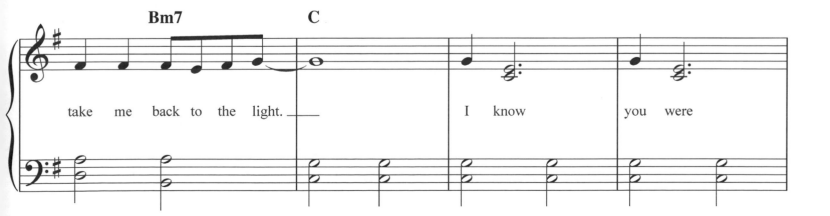

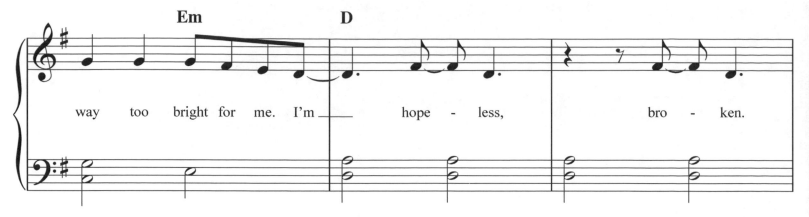

way too bright for me. I'm _____ hope - less, bro - ken.

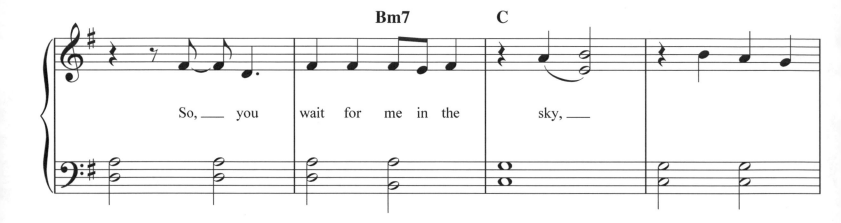

So, _____ you wait for me in the sky, _____

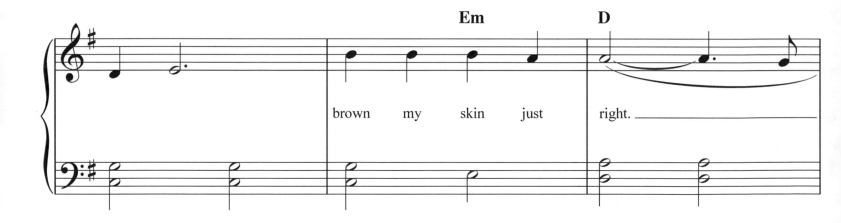

brown my skin just right. _____

_____ You're so gold - en.

(Dah dah dah dah dah dah dah dah dah dah dah dah dah.)

You're so bro - ken. ___ (Dah dah dah dah.) I'm out of my head ___ and I know ___

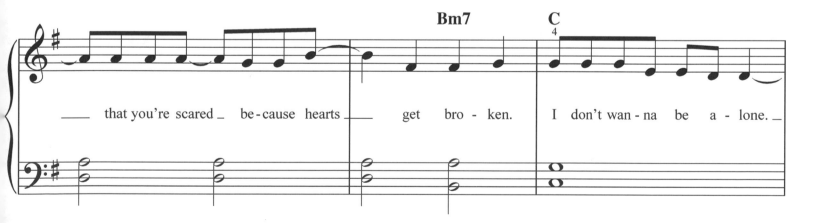

___ that you're scared ___ be-cause hearts ___ get bro - ken. I don't wan - na be a - lone. ___

___ I don't wan - na be a - lone ___ when it

(Dah dah dah dah dah dah dah dah dah dah dah dah dah.)

You're so gold - en. (Dah dah dah dah.) I don't wan - na be a - lone.

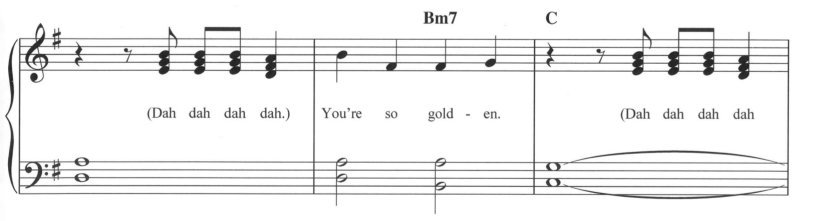

(Dah dah dah dah.) You're so gold - en. (Dah dah dah dah

dah dah dah dah dah dah dah dah dah.) You're so gold - en. (Dah dah dah dah.)

To Coda ⊕

Bm7

Out of my head _ and I know _ that you're scared _ be-cause hearts _ get bro - ken.

C

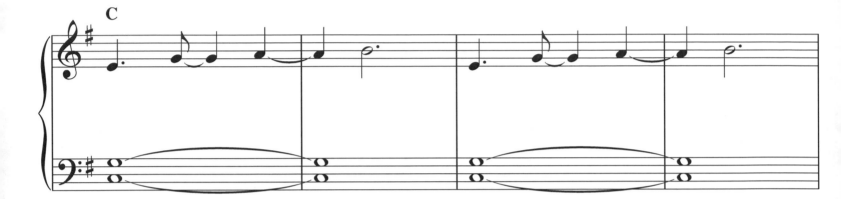

D

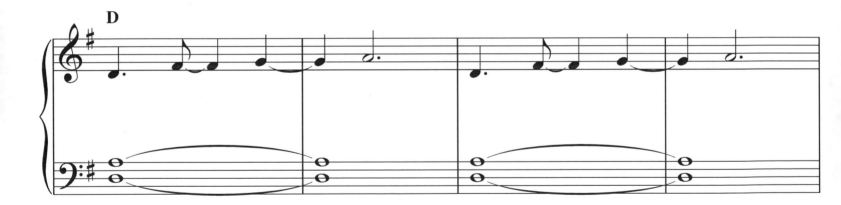

C

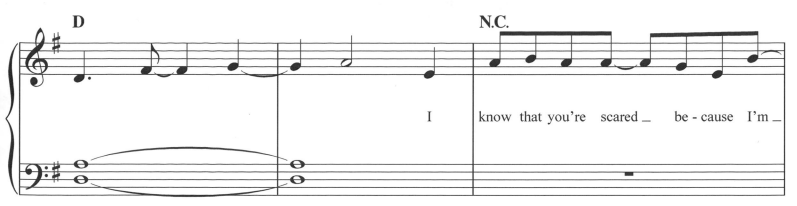

I know that you're scared _ be-cause I'm _

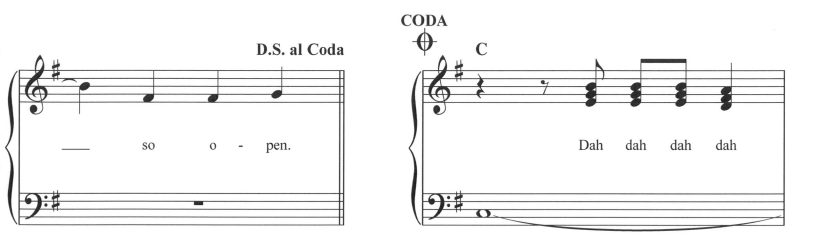

_ so o - pen.

Dah dah dah dah

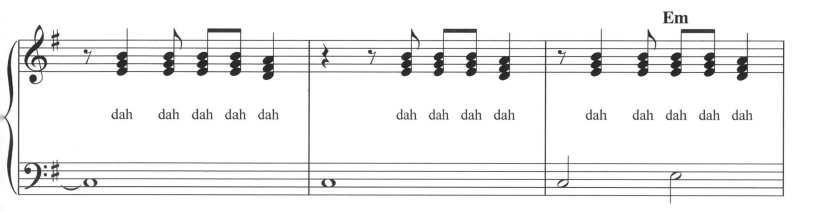

dah dah dah dah dah

dah dah dah dah

dah dah dah dah dah

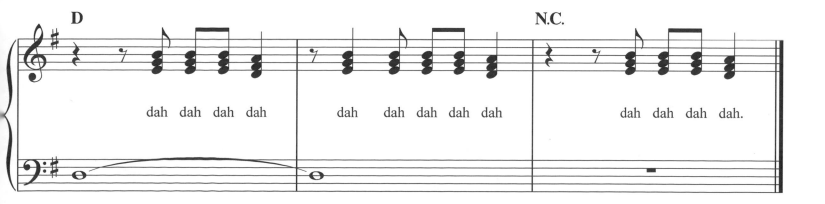

dah dah dah dah

dah dah dah dah dah

dah dah dah dah.

KIWI

Words and Music by HARRY STYLES,
JEFF BHASKER, TYLER JOHNSON,
ALEX SALIBIAN, MITCH ROWLAND
and RYAN NASCI

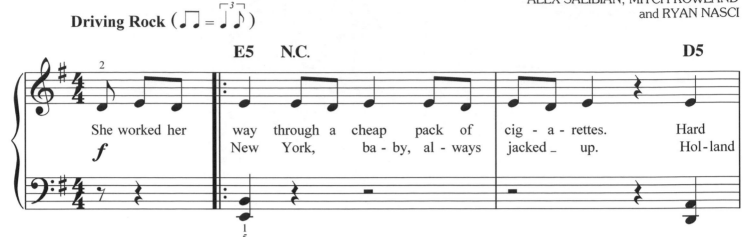

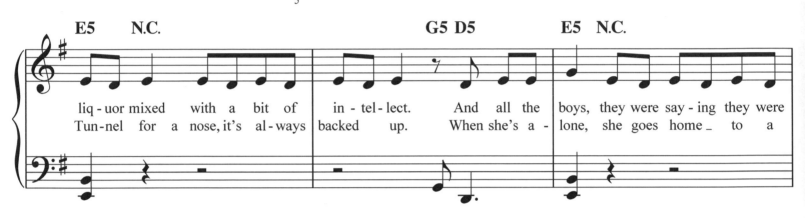

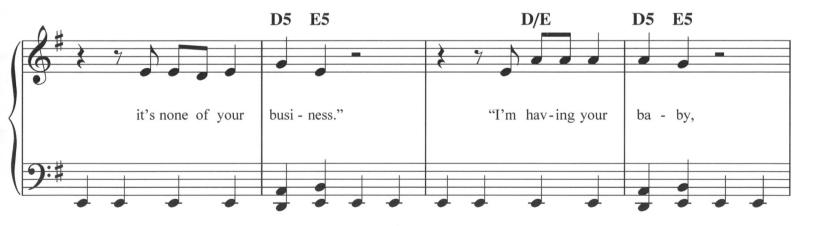

ba - by,   it's none of your   busi - ness."   "I'm hav-ing your

ba - by,   it's none of your,   it's none of your."

It's

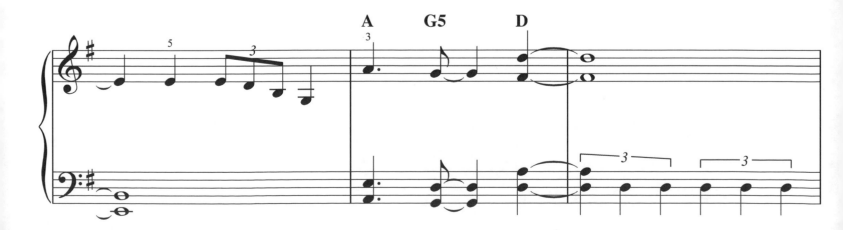

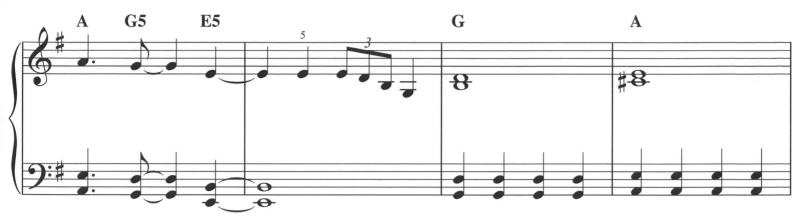

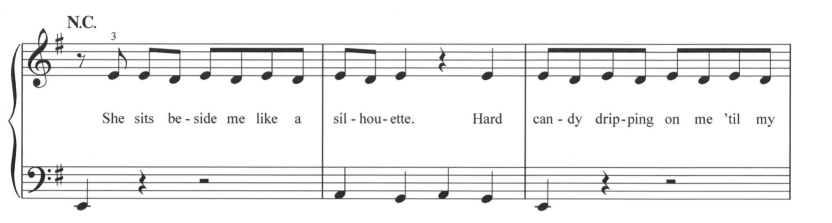

She sits be-side me like a sil-hou-ette. Hard can-dy drip-ping on me 'til my

feet are wet. And now she's all o-ver me, it's like I paid for it, it's like I

paid for it. I'm gon-na pay for this.

It's none of your, it's none of your... "I'm hav-ing your

ba - by, it's none of your busi - ness."

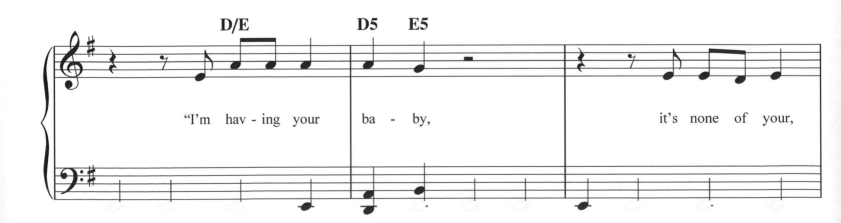

"I'm hav-ing your ba - by, it's none of your,

busi - ness." "I'm hav - ing your ba - by, hey,

it's none of your busi - ness." "Hav - ing your

ba - by. _____ It's none of your busi - ness."

SIGN OF THE TIMES

Words and Music by HARRY STYLES,
JEFF BHASKER, MITCH ROWLAND,
RYAN NASCI, ALEX SALIBIAN
and TYLER JOHNSON

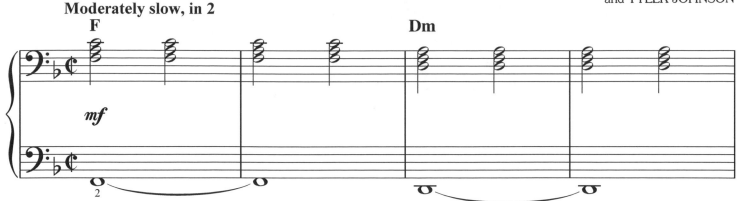

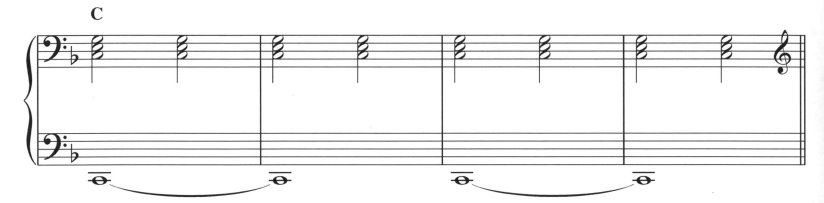

Just stop your cry - ing; it's a sign of the times.
Just stop your cry - ing, have the time of your life.

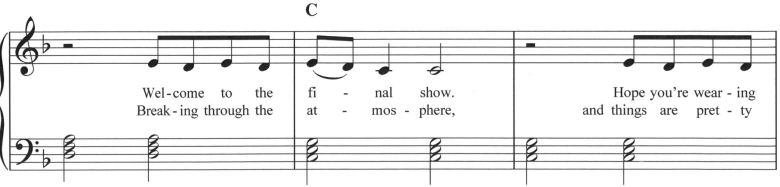

Wel - come to the fi - nal show. Hope you're wear - ing
Break - ing through the at - mos - phere, and things are pret - ty

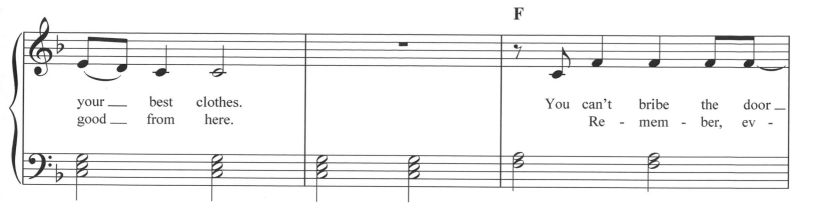

your ___ best clothes.
good ___ from here.

F

You can't bribe the door ___
Re - mem - ber, ev -

Dm

___ on your way to the sky. ___
- 'ry - thing will be al - right. ___

You look pret - ty
We can meet a -

C

good ___ down here,
gain ___ some - where,

but you ain't real - ly
some - where far a -

good. ___
way ___ from here.

F

We nev - er learn; we've been here be - fore.

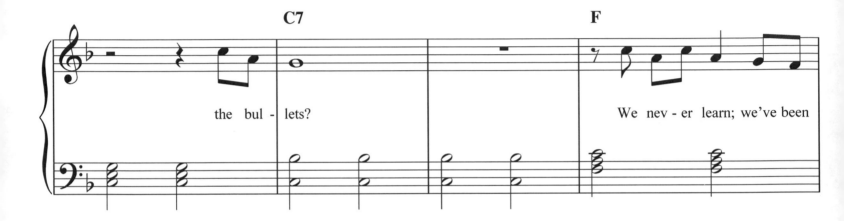

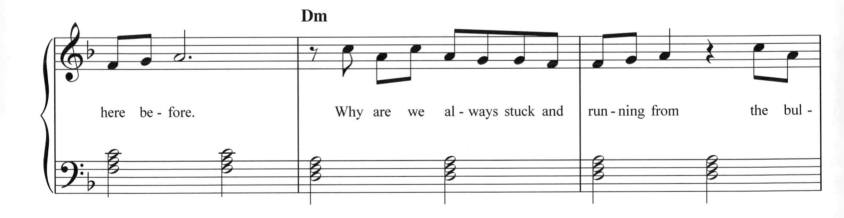

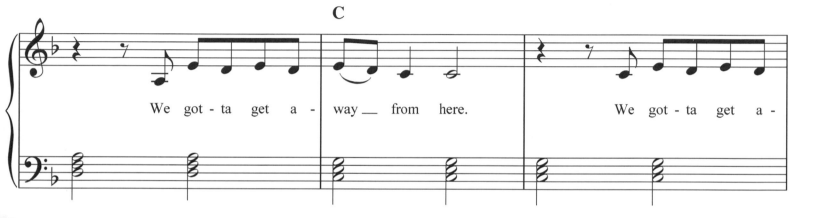

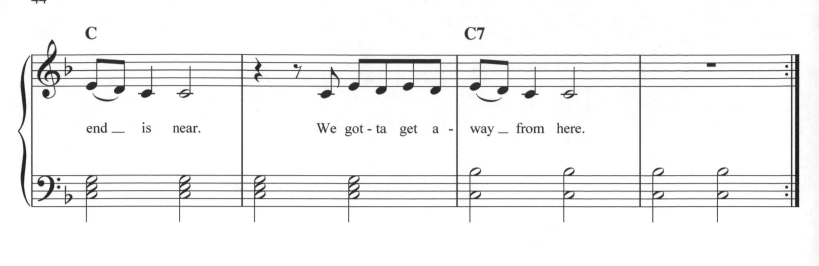

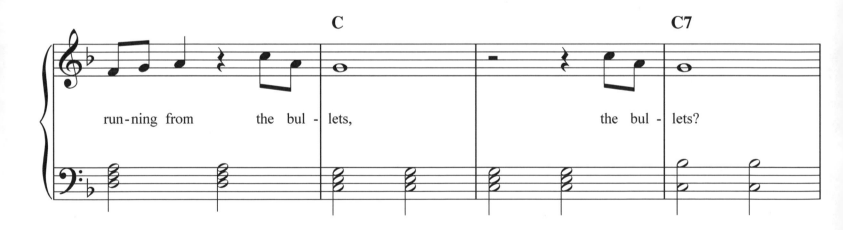

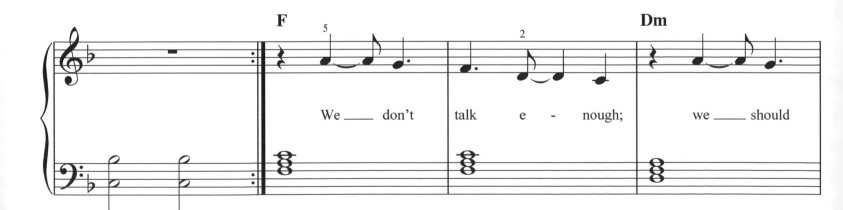

We got-ta get a - way. ___ We got to get a-

way. ___ We got to get a - way. ___

We got to get a - way. ___ We got to get a-

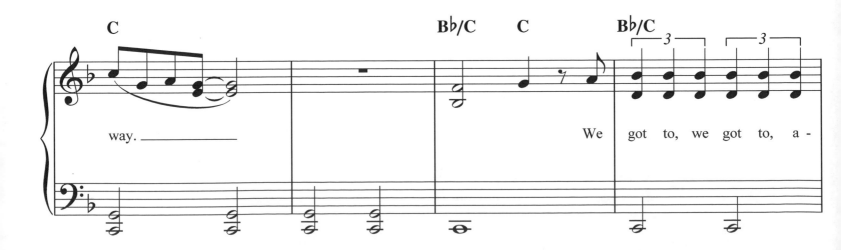

way. ___ We got to, we got to, a-

way. We got to, we got to, a - way. We

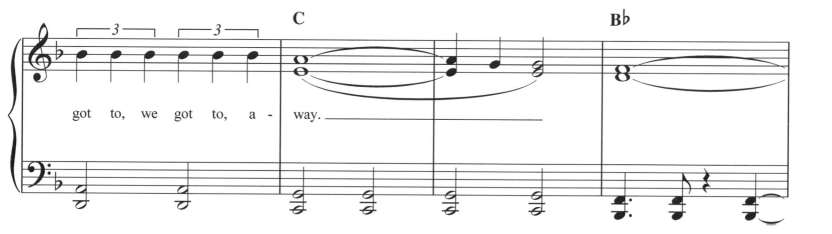

got to, we got to, a - way. _____

SWEET CREATURE

Words and Music by HARRY STYLES
and THOMAS HULL

Acoustic Ballad

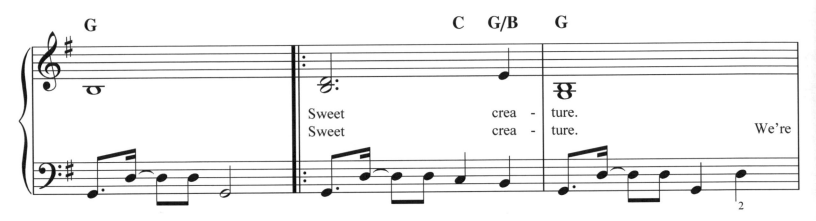

Sweet   crea - ture.
Sweet   crea - ture.   We're

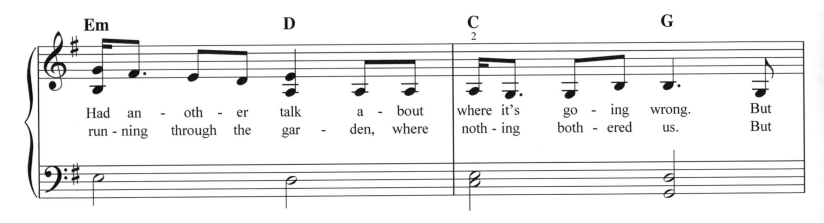

Had an - oth - er talk a - bout   where it's go - ing wrong.   But
run - ning through the gar - den, where   noth - ing both - ered us.   But

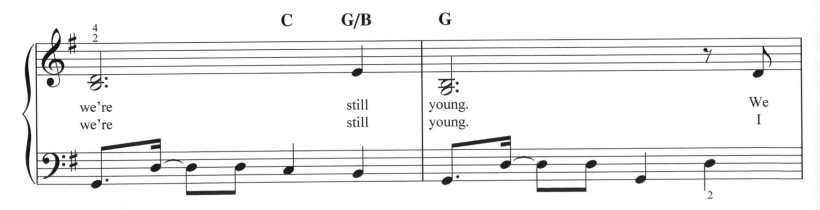

we're   still   young.   We
we're   still   young.   I

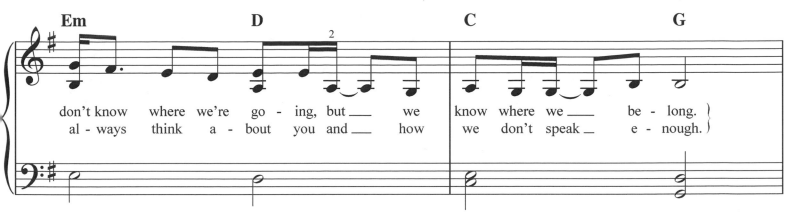

don't know where we're go - ing, but ___ we know where we ___ be - long.
al - ways think a - bout you and ___ how we don't speak ___ e - nough.

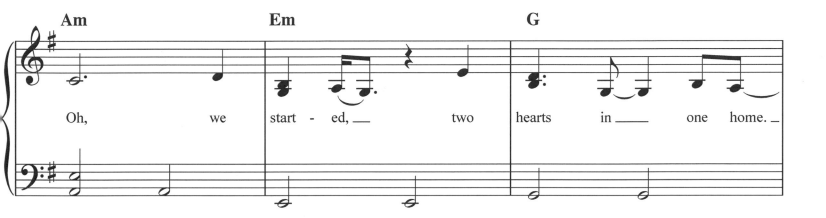

Oh, we start - ed, ___ two hearts in ___ one home. ___

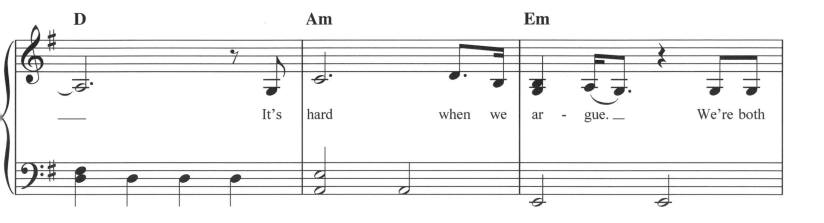

___ It's hard when we ar - gue. ___ We're both

stub - born, I ___ know. ___ But, oh, ___ sweet crea -

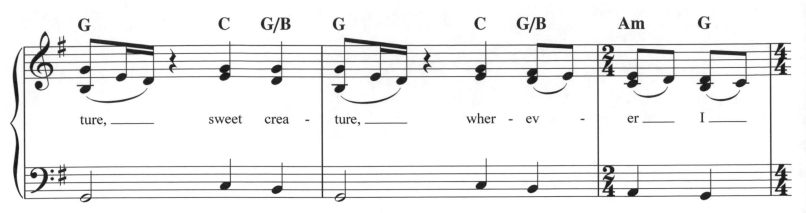

ture, _____ sweet crea - ture, _____ wher - ev - er _____ I _____

go, you bring _ me home. _____ Sweet crea -

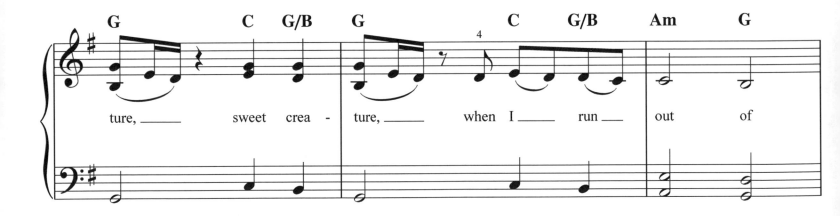

ture, _____ sweet crea - ture, _____ when I _____ run _____ out of

road, you bring _ me home. _ (Ooh, _____ ooh.) _____

home. ____ (Ooh, ____ ooh. ____ Ooh, ____

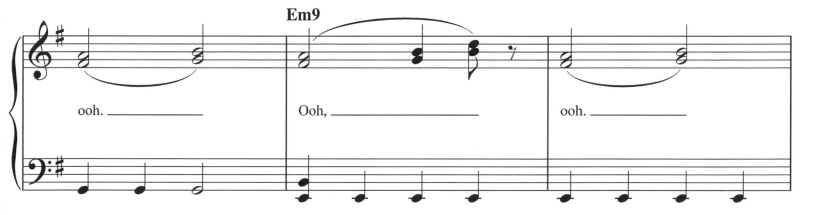

ooh. ____ Ooh, ____ ooh. ____

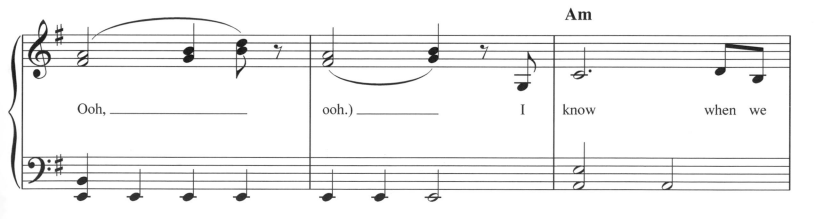

Ooh, ____ ooh.) ____ I know when we

start - ed, just two hearts in ____ one ____ home. It gets

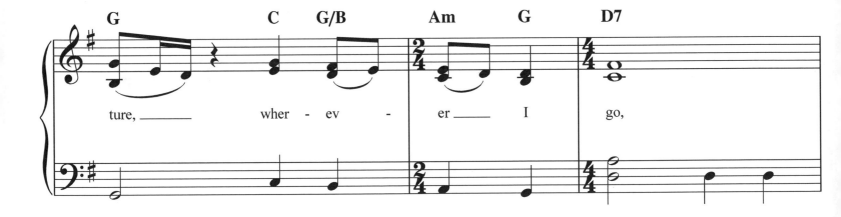

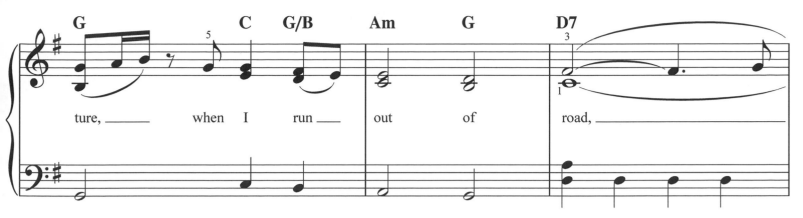

ture, _____ when I run ___ out of road, _____ ____

___ you bring _ me home.

You bring _ me home. __ (Ooh, ___

ooh. _____ Ooh, _____ ooh.) _____

TWO GHOSTS

Words and Music by HARRY STYLES,
TYLER JOHNSON, JOHN RYAN,
JULIAN BUNETTA and MITCH ROWLAND

Moderately slow Ballad

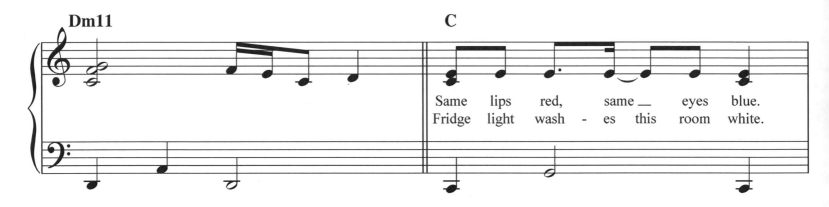

Same lips red, same __ eyes blue.
Fridge light wash - es this room white.

Same white shirt, cou - ple more tat - toos.
Moon danc - es o - ver your __ good side.

It's not you and it's not me. __
This was all we used to need. __

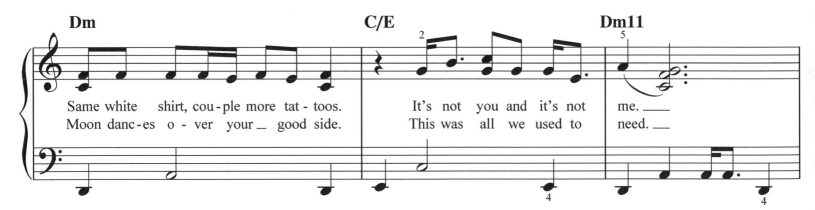

Tastes so sweet, looks so real. __
Tongue tied like I've nev - er known. __

Sounds like some - thin' that I used to feel __
Tell - in' those stor - ies we al - rea - dy told. __

we're not ___ who we used to be. ___ We're not ___

___ who we used to be. ___ We're just two ghosts swim-min' in a glass half emp - ty, ___

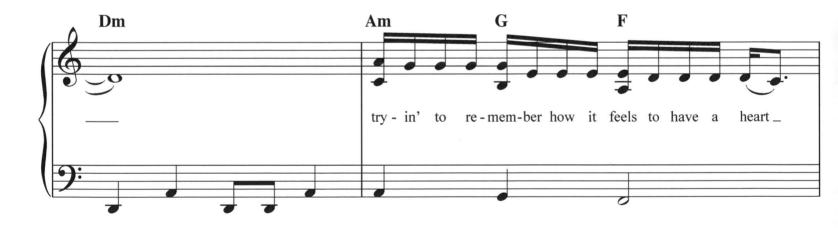

___ try - in' to re-mem-ber how it feels to have a heart ___

beat.

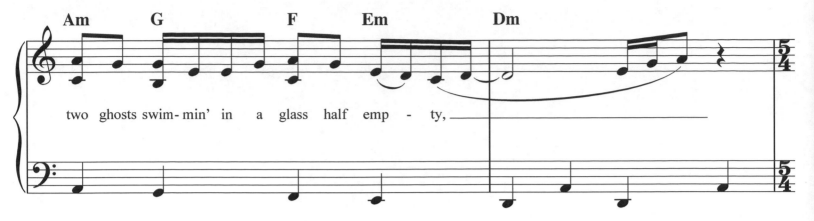

two ghosts swim- min' in a glass half emp - ty,

try- in' to re-mem-ber how it feels to have a heart beat.

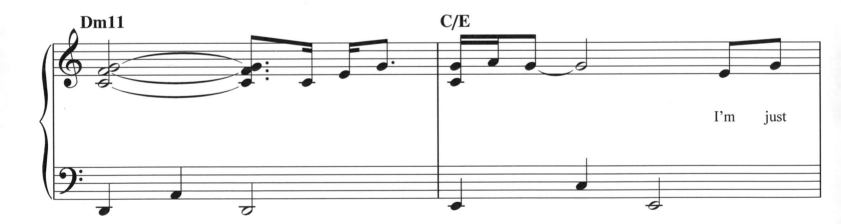

I'm just

try - in' to re-mem-ber how it feels to have a heart beat.

WATERMELON SUGAR

Words and Music by HARRY STYLES,
THOMAS HULL, MITCHELL ROWLAND
and TYLER JOHNSON

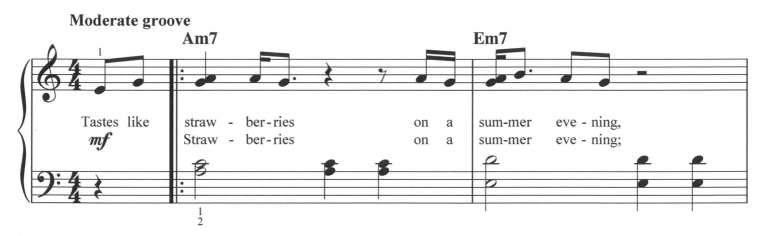

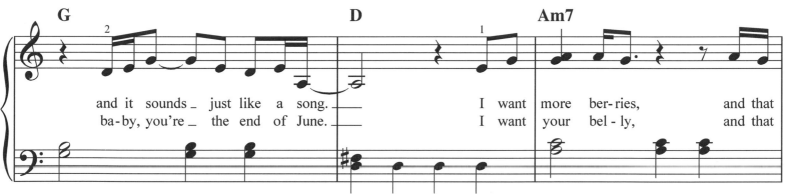

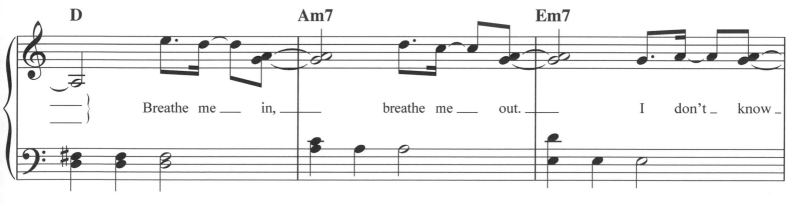

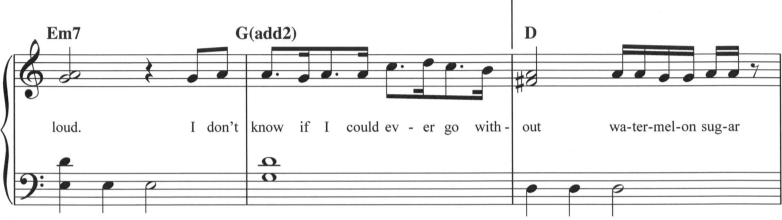

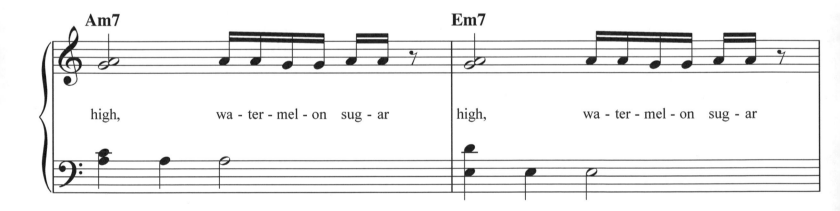

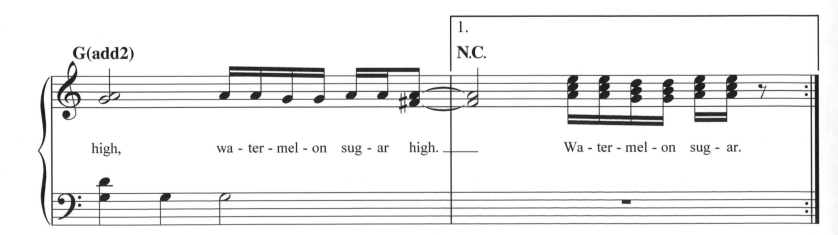

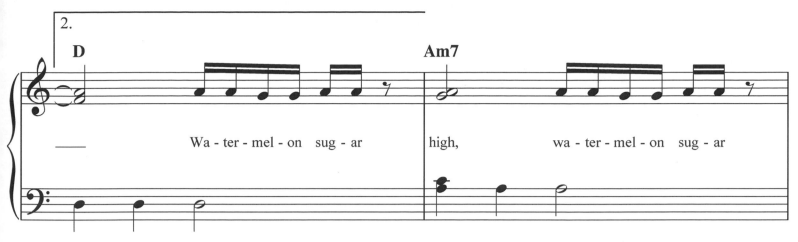

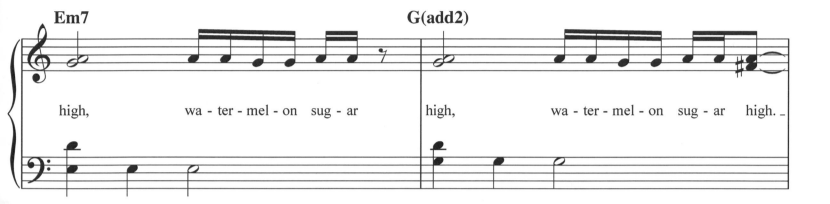

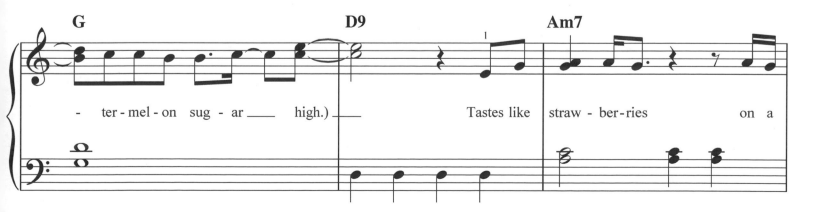

sum - mer eve - ning; and it sounds __ just like a song. __

__ I want your bel - ly, and that sum-mer feel - ing. I don't

know if I could ev - er go with - out wa - ter - mel - on sug - ar

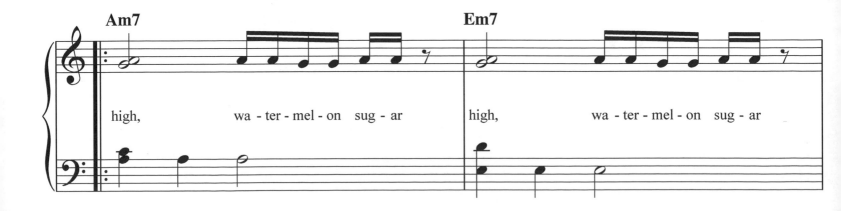

high, wa - ter - mel - on sug - ar high, wa - ter - mel - on sug - ar

high, wa - ter - mel - on sug - ar high. _____ Wa - ter - mel - on sug - ar.

_____ (I _____ just wan - na taste it, I _____ just wan - na taste it, wa -

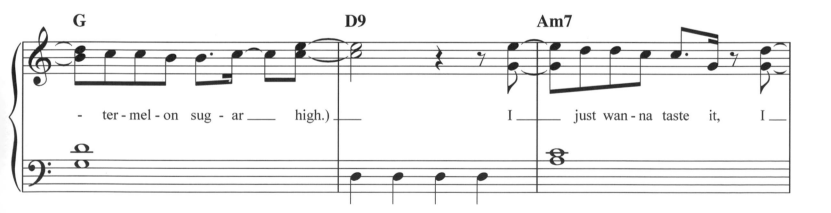

- ter - mel - on sug - ar _____ high.) _____ I _____ just wan - na taste it, I _____

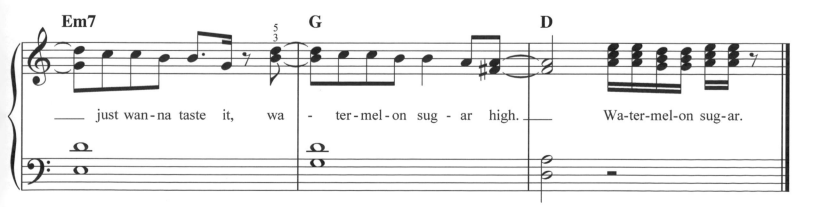

_____ just wan - na taste it, wa - ter - mel - on sug - ar high. _____ Wa - ter - mel - on sug - ar.